gather

EASY GLUTEN FREE MEALS
FOR THE WHOLE FAMILY

Raquel Bosustow

To the man of my life, Scott Krywulycz,
who has supported me endlessly for over 33 years
in every adventure I take on.

Probably because they all have to do with food – and he is fed well!

Here's what you need to know about this cookbook

I write simple recipes that are delicious and easy to follow. My meals may be simple, but they're packed with flavour and guaranteed to impress. Plus, they don't require a lot of time in the kitchen—perfect for busy schedules.

That means happy family and friends.

Gluten-free all the way.

I don't like to measure – this can drive some people crazy, especially the perfectionists who measure every part of a recipe. However, writing a cookbook has made me quite accurate. But my wish for you is to learn to be rustic and add that extra pinch of curry powder or garlic if you feel the meal requires it.

Cooking should be fun and creative. Don't be afraid to experiment with flavours and trust your instincts. Over time, you'll develop a sense of what works well together.

Don't get too caught up in the details when it comes to cooking. Feel free to chop your onions however you like, sprinkle herbs with your own unique flair, and slice or dice your veggies to your preference. The result will always be delicious!

Remember to have fun and let your creativity shine through.

However, there are some rules: Only use olive oil or sesame oil as per the recipe. Never use vegetable oil, and only cook with raw sugar, not refined white sugar.

Now, pour yourself a glass of wine and get those ingredients ready!

I'm super excited to take you on this journey.

Simply. Healthy. Happy.

Let's do this!

Table of Contents

At a Glance...

 15

 17

 19

 47

 49

 59

 71

 73

 85

Let's get Inspired!

 87

 89

 91

 93

 99

 101

 107

 111

 113

Hearty Meals To Fill You Up!

As a mum of a gluten free family, I'm on a mission to find hearty meals to feed my growing kids!

I love finding a recipe, swapping out the ingredients, cooking up a storm, and perfecting it to impress my favourite people.

Eating as a family is so important, but it's not always easy to do as life changes. Sunday nights are our ritual of coming together around the table, whether it's the five of us, my brother-in-law and my nieces, or friends of friends and family.

People are amazed at how effortlessly I can create a huge buffet of goodness, and the non gluten free people wouldn't even know they're eating gluten free food.

I often sit back and just enjoy the moment of watching everyone serve themselves and get excited about eating. Food always brings people together.

Let's create family memories for you – which recipe will you choose first?

Almond Crusted Chicken Breast

Make a large batch, as this will go quickly! I serve it with garlic mashed potatoes and lots of veggies. This recipe seems so simple but that's where the magic is – simple, delicious ingredients will make the perfect dish to cook and to eat! It's also super healthy and the texture is incredibly addictive.

Ingredients

1 cup (150g) roasted, unsalted almonds
1 clove of garlic
2 tbsp dried oregano
2 tbsp olive oil
½ tsp sea salt
4 x 150g free-range chicken breasts, flattened like schnitzels
1 tbsp olive oil, for frying
1 cup each of mixed broccoli, peas, beans, and zucchini, diced
1 handful of baby spinach
2 tbsp lemon juice

Instructions

1. Heat the oven to 200°C / 400°F / Gas 6.

2. In a food processor, pulse the almonds, garlic, oregano, and olive oil with the sea salt until combined and roughly chopped.

3. Pat the almond mixture onto the chicken breasts and place them on a baking tray lined with baking paper.

4. Roast in the preheated oven for 15 to 18 minutes. The best way to check if the chicken is cooked through is to slice into the thickest part.

5. Add 1 tablespoon of olive oil to a pan. Toss your green veggies for 2 minutes.

6. Transfer the veggies to a bowl and toss through the baby spinach. Add a squeeze of lemon and a pinch of salt. Combine everything on your plate and enjoy!

I like to place this dish in a large bowl for everyone to help themselves. Squeeze some lemon over it all, and add crushed nuts, fresh coriander, and some chilli to make it as spicy as you like.

My Famous Pad Thai

My delicious Pad Thai recipe will fill hungry tummies and is always a winner! It's super easy to make and perfect for sharing. We all want healthy, quick meals mid-week, and my mission is to encourage you to cook with ease. The peanut butter is the key ingredient, adding a nutty taste without dominating the dish.

Ingredients

¼ cup tamari
½ cup peanut butter
1 tbsp brown sugar
1 BBQ chicken, cooked
250g packet of rice noodles
1 carrot, cut into sticks
1 handful of green beans, sliced
4 spring onions, chopped
1 tsp crushed garlic
¼ cup sesame oil
250g bean sprouts
1 cup crushed peanuts
Juice of a lemon
Small bunch of fresh coriander
Chilli flakes, to taste

Instructions

1. Combine tamari, peanut butter, brown sugar, and 2 tablespoons of water. Set aside.

2. Take the meat off the BBQ chicken and place it in a bowl.

3. Cook the rice noodles according to packet instructions.

4. Stir fry the veggies with garlic in the sesame oil. Add them to the bowl with the cooked rice noodles and bean sprouts.

5. Add the sauce, crushed peanuts, lemon juice, coriander and chilli flakes and toss everything together. Serve immediately.

Prawn & Egg Fried Rice

I make a big batch of this on holidays and leave it in the fridge to fill up the kids! I love that this is a healthy, filling option instead of a packet of chips or sugary treats. It's easy to reheat in a frypan or enjoy cold.

Ingredients

2 ½ tbsp sesame oil
2 eggs, lightly beaten
2 small red chillies, seeds removed, chopped
6 spring onions, finely shredded
3 garlic cloves, finely chopped
Chopped veg (whatever you have in the fridge)
400g peeled green prawns, tails intact
200g medium–grain rice, cooked to packet instructions
1/3 cup (80ml) tamari
1 tbsp sweet chilli sauce
1 cup (120g) frozen peas
Coriander leaves and lime wedges (optional)

Instructions

1. Heat 1 tablespoon of sesame oil in a wok or large frypan over medium-high heat. Add the eggs and cook, stirring, for 1-2 minutes until softly scrambled. Remove the eggs from the pan and set aside.

2. Add the remaining sesame oil to the pan, then cook the chillies, spring onions, and garlic, stirring, for 1 minute or until fragrant. Add extra veg to taste and cook until beginning to soften.

3. Add the prawns and cook for 2-3 minutes until cooked through.

4. Return the eggs to the pan with the rice, tamari, sweet chilli sauce, and peas. Cook, stirring, for 2-3 minutes to warm through.

5. Garnish with coriander and lime wedges.

Slow Cooked Italian Lamb Shanks

I love making this dish on Sunday afternoons at home. It's my favourite time of the week, enjoying the cozy kitchen, weekend sports on TV, and a glass of wine. This is a perfect family meal and makes plenty of leftovers for the week ahead.

Ingredients

2 tbsp olive oil
4 lamb shanks
1 red onion, diced
3 celery sticks, diced
2 tbsp tomato paste
1 cup (250ml) red wine
2 cups (500ml) chicken stock
5 cloves garlic, crushed
1 tbsp lemon zest, finely grated
2 cups arborio rice, cooked
parsley or basil
grated Parmesan cheese

Instructions

1. Heat the oven to 180°C / 350°F /Gas 4.

2. Add oil to a large oven-proof frying pan, brown the lamb shanks, then add the diced vegetables and tomato paste. Cook for a few minutes until softened.

3. Pour in the red wine and chicken stock, then add the garlic and lemon zest. Top up with water to cover the shanks.

4. Cover with foil and roast for 90 minutes at 180°C in the preheated oven. You may need to top up with water along the way.

5. After 60 minutes, cook the rice following the packet instructions. Once the rice and shanks are cooked, remove the shanks from the pan and shred the meat.

6. Add the shredded meat to the liquid and mix in the cooked rice. Serve in individual bowls with a sprinkle of fresh herbs such as parsley or basil. Add a bowl of grated Parmesan on the side and enjoy with a full-bodied red wine!

Secret Italian Nonna Dishes

I was 18 when my Nonna passed away. I had just met my husband, Scott.

As a little girl, we would go to her house every Sunday for lunch. My brothers and I would always eat at the table, then go into the TV room to watch Elvis Presley movies and munch on Italian sweets.

All of my comfort foods come from this time.

When my daughter Hanna was 18 months old, I took her on a plane to Italy. Gosh, I can't believe I did that on my own! It was one of the most memorable trips of my life.

After arriving in Italy, we met my parents, who were on a trip themselves, and visited the village of Arten, where my mum was born. According to Mum, it hasn't changed much – just a simple village with the delicious waft of garlic and onion coming from every household.

We also visited my mum's great-aunt, Zia Monica Maria. My dad, mum, brother, Hanna and I spent the entire day without speaking English (though my dad only pretends to speak Italian). My poor brother had to finish all the grappa because we couldn't handle it!

Zia Monica Maria taught me to make authentic Bolognese sauce with only four ingredients. The flavour was beyond anything I had tasted before. It was then that I learned to enjoy the art of simple cooking. At this very long lunch, we grazed on eight courses of incredible Italian food and left my aunt's house feeling very, very happy.

You are lucky – as I am going to share this secret family recipe later on in the book.... it's my gift to you!

I recently visited a medium where my Nonna came through. It blew me away as the medium called her by name – Maria.

My Nonna told me how proud she is of my cooking and loves that I cook with my hands just like her.

As tears fell down my face, I felt a beautiful energy in this space. She also asked me why there's no photo of her in my kitchen!

Well, Nonna, here is your photo and yes, it's in my kitchen!

Nonna's Spinach & Ricotta Gnocchi
with homemade tomato sauce

A taste of Italy right here and right now – worth the time! My Nonna was and is my cooking hero. Although I was only little and then in my teens before she passed away, I would admire her rustic cooking with simple ingredients that created so much flavour.

Ingredients

TOMATO SAUCE:
1 tbsp olive oil
2 onions, finely chopped
6 large tomatoes, chopped
Bunch of basil
½ cup (125ml) red wine
2 tbsp tomato paste

GNOCCHI:
1kg large white potatoes, cleaned
200g baby spinach
350g ricotta
2 eggs
125g Parmesan, grated
100g gluten-free plain flour

Instructions

1. Heat the oven to 180°C / 350°F / Gas 4. Roast the potatoes until soft, about 45 minutes. Allow to cool for a few minutes, then scoop out the middle, leaving the skins. (Tip: Fry up the skins for the kids to nibble on!)

2. To make the sauce, heat olive oil in a frypan and sauté the onions and garlic. Add the tomatoes and remaining ingredients, bring to a boil, then simmer for 15 minutes on low heat.

3. In a bowl, add the scooped-out potatoes and all remaining ingredients. Combine well.

4. Spread some flour on a surface, take a handful of the mixture, and roll it into a long cigar-shaped roll. Dice into 3 cm pieces and set aside on plates.

5. Bring a large pot of water to a boil and add 10 gnocchi at a time. Once they float, they are cooked.

6. Combine the gnocchi with the sauce and enjoy!

Serve with roasted
potatoes
and a fresh salad.

Add a wedge of lemon
for a zesty finish.

Healthy Chicken Parmigiana

A winner-winner chicken dinner for all lovers of this traditional meal. You wouldn't even know it's gluten-free! I discovered this secret recipe years ago, in search of an alternative to highly processed store-bought gluten-free crumbs. You can make up the dry mixture and keep it in your fridge to use again and again.

Ingredients

4 chicken breasts (150g each)
1 cup (200g) ricotta
1 handful of baby spinach
1 red onion, diced
Garlic (to taste)
1 cup (150g) polenta
1 cup (150g) almond meal
1 pinch of salt
1 tsp oregano
1 cup (250ml) Greek yoghurt
1 cup (250ml) passata
1 cup mozzarella
Olive oil spray

Instructions

1. Heat the oven to 180°C / 350°F / Gas 4.

2. Make a slit in each chicken breast. Combine ricotta, baby spinach, red onion, garlic and a pinch of salt. Stuff each breast with this mixture.

3. Combine polenta, almond meal, salt, and oregano in a bowl. Place some yoghurt in a separate dish.

4. Dunk each chicken breast in yoghurt first, then coat it with the crumbing mixture.

5. Place the chicken breasts on a baking tray and lightly coat them with a spray of olive oil. Bake in the preheated oven for 30 minutes.

6. Take the chicken breasts out of the oven, top with passata and grated mozzarella. Bake for 10 more minutes to melt the cheese.

The chunk of Parmesan cheese rind is the hero of this delicious soup, and will bring all the wonderfully rustic flavours to life.

Authentic Minestrone Soup

This is a hug in a bowl. My kids will even eat it for breakfast! This was definitely my Nonna's favourite soup, and I loved enjoying it at her kitchen table sitting on yellow chairs. There was always extra Parmesan to stir through and watch the melting magic.

Ingredients

1 dash of olive oil
1 onion, diced
5 large cloves of garlic, diced
3 carrots, cleaned and diced
200g pancetta, sliced
1 zucchini, diced
1 cup fresh green beans,
cut into ½ inch pieces
2 white potatoes, diced
1½ cups spinach, chopped
1 cup fresh cabbage, chopped
2 tins Italian diced tomatoes
1 tin cannellini beans, drained
1 big chunk of Parmesan rind
2 litres chicken or veggie stock
1 cup (200g) gluten-free pasta
1 bunch flat-leaf parsley, chopped
Freshly grated Parmesan

Instructions

1. In a large pot, heat the oil and add the onion, garlic, carrots, and pancetta. Gently sauté for about 5 minutes.

2. Add the zucchini, beans, potatoes, spinach, cabbage, tomatoes, cannellini beans, and the Parmesan cheese rind. Fill up the pot with chicken or vegetable stock.

3. Place the lid on the pot and cook for 30 minutes.

4. Add the pasta to the hot soup and cook with the lid off until the pasta is 'al dente'.

5. Garnish with parsley and freshly grated Parmesan cheese.

Gluten-Free Gnocchi

My mum taught our kids how to make gnocchi; they are now even better at it than I am! They know exactly how the mixture should feel to create the best gnocchi – and so will you after a couple of times. You'll know when the mixture is perfect by the texture (like playdough), not too sticky, not too dry.

Ingredients

4 kg unpeeled white potatoes
4 eggs
1–2 cups gluten–free flour
Sea salt

Instructions

1. Preheat the oven to 200°C / 400°F / Gas 6. Bake the potatoes for about 50 minutes until tender when pierced with a knife. Let them cool for about 10 minutes until easily handled.

2. Peel the potatoes and pass them through a ricer or food mill into a large bowl. Make a well in the mashed potatoes with a wooden spoon and crack in the eggs and mix well.

3. Gradually add flour to the potato mixture and stir until a soft dough has formed.

4. Cut the dough into 4 equal parts with a knife.

5. Dust the kitchen bench with gluten-free flour to keep the dough from sticking. Roll out one piece of dough at a time into a rope about 1 inch in diameter. Cut into 2.5 cm gnocchi. Gently roll each one with the back of a fork to create ridges. Repeat with the remaining dough.

6. Bring a large pot of salted water to the boil. Add gnocchi in batches and cook, without stirring, until they float to the top, about 2 minutes.

Serve these gnocchi with either homemade pesto or a good pesto from a jar.

I love to serve them on a platter, drizzle over some pesto, squeeze of lemon, and a handful of Parmesan cheese.

Finish off with a sprinkle of salt. Delicious!

Try using other fresh herbs in pesto! Rocket and coriander both make a beautiful bright green sauce.

Homemade Basil Pesto

Add a flavour boost to your meals with my homemade basil pesto. Combining the freshness of basil with the richness of cashews or pine nuts, garlic, Parmesan, and olive oil, it's a must-have for any kitchen.

Ingredients

1 large bunch fresh basil
1 handful baby spinach
2 cloves of garlic
2 tbsp cashews or pine nuts
1 handful of grated Parmesan
Pinch of salt
¼ cup of olive oil

Instructions

1. Give the basil and spinach a good wash and pat dry.

2. Blitz all ingredients together in a food processor until smooth.

3. If not using immediately, transfer to clean glass jars, cover with a layer of olive oil and store in the fridge.

37

Happy Detoxing

Let's be clear here:

Detoxing does not mean living off air.

By removing heavy foods, gluten, dairy, sugar, acid, and toxins, you allow your digestive system to rest, restore, and repair itself.

I recommend including a 'Detox Week' once a quarter, as the seasons change. Not only will your body love it, but mentally, you'll have more clarity, sleep better, and have more energy.

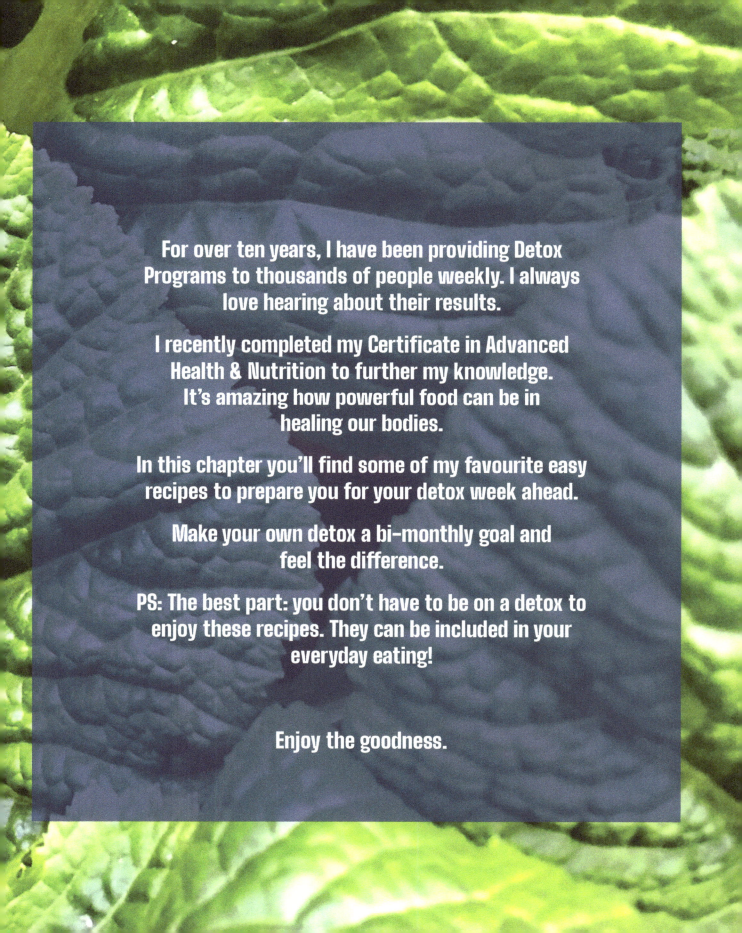

For over ten years, I have been providing Detox Programs to thousands of people weekly. I always love hearing about their results.

I recently completed my Certificate in Advanced Health & Nutrition to further my knowledge. It's amazing how powerful food can be in healing our bodies.

In this chapter you'll find some of my favourite easy recipes to prepare you for your detox week ahead.

Make your own detox a bi-monthly goal and feel the difference.

PS: The best part: you don't have to be on a detox to enjoy these recipes. They can be included in your everyday eating!

Enjoy the goodness.

Green Machine Detox Chicken Salad

Green – green – green! So many of us are acidic due to our intake of coffee, alcohol, and sugars. The idea of a detox is to bring as much alkalinity into our food intake as possible. This means as much green as possible! I love this recipe because you can include all of the ingredients, plus whatever else you have in the fridge!

Ingredients

1 x 200g chicken breast
1 slice of lemon
Mixed lettuce (about a handful)
1 carrot, sliced
½ avocado, sliced
1 cucumber, sliced
1 celery stalk, sliced
1 cup of beans, sliced
½ cup raw broccoli, sliced
1 handful of sunflower seeds

DRESSING
In a jar, add:
2 tbsp olive oil
2 tbsp white wine vinegar
1 pinch of fresh parsley
½ a lemon, squeezed

Instructions

1. Place the chicken breast in a pot and cover it with water. Add a slice of lemon, bring to a boil, then reduce heat to low. Partly cover the pot and simmer for 5-8 minutes.

2. Turn the heat off and leave the chicken in the hot water for another 10 minutes until thoroughly cooked. Remove from the poaching liquid and allow to cool.

3. Throw all remaining ingredients except the chicken in a bowl.

4. Slice the chicken breast thinly and add to the salad bowl.

5. Shake the jar with the dressing ingredients and toss through the salad.

Tuna Salad Lettuce Wraps

This is a quick and easy lunch that takes no more than 5 minutes to make. It seems simple, yet the flavours are incredible together. This is my husband's go-to lunch at least one a week, and he often has to make triple the recipe as we all crave the crunch of this lettuce cup masterpiece!

Ingredients

1 can of tuna in olive oil, 350g
¼ red onion, diced
1 celery stalk, finely sliced
¼ cup capers
1 teaspoon Dijon mustard
1 handful of chopped dill
2–3 Cos lettuces

Instructions

1. Mix all ingredients except the lettuce in a large bowl until well combined. Keep the mixture in the fridge, covered, until ready to serve.

2. Give the lettuce a good wash, then separate into individual leaves.

3. Spoon the tuna mixture into lettuce cups and enjoy!

For extra flavour, marinate the salmon in tamari for 15 minutes before cooking.

Gingered Salmon Stir Fry

When I first became gluten-free 25 years ago, there was no substitute for Asian sauces. Many years later, gluten-free soy sauce, also known as tamari, was invented and it's the best! It's a lighter flavour than standard soy, and can be found in most supermarkets. This should be a staple in your fridge!

Ingredients

1 tbsp sesame oil
150g salmon fillet,
cut into chunks
½ cup snow peas, thinly sliced
1 carrot, sliced
3 shallots, sliced
2 tbsp ginger, finely grated
1 bok choy, sliced
1 garlic clove, crushed
Gluten-free tamari sauce
¼ cup almonds, chopped
Optional: coriander and chilli

Instructions

1. Heat a pan on high heat and add the sesame oil. Once hot, add the salmon, skin side down. It will be sizzling and smelling fabulous.

2. After two minutes, turn the salmon over to the other side. Add ¼ cup of water and then place the lid on. This will steam through the centre of the salmon to cook it evenly.

3. After flipping the salmon for the first time, add the snow peas, carrots, shallots, ginger, bok choy, and garlic.

4. Cook until fragrant and the vegetables are tender. Then add a few splashes of tamari and place the lid on to steam for one minute.

5. Serve in a bowl or on a plate. Sprinkle with almonds, chopped coriander, and chopped chilli to your liking.

Asian-Style Steamed Fish

with Spring Onion and Ginger

Sometimes, the simplest ingredients create the most delicious dishes! I love to cook this midweek for dinner when there's no time to cook up a feast. It's a huge dose of protein and omega-3 goodness.

Ingredients

4 x 150g white fish fillets
1 tbsp light soy sauce
1 tsp sesame oil
½ tsp raw sugar
1 tbsp rice vinegar
3cm piece of ginger,
finely shredded
1 each long red and green chilli,
seeds removed,
thinly sliced
6 spring onions, finely shredded
Coriander leaves
Steamed rice, to serve

Instructions

1. Place a plate inside a bamboo steamer and lay the fish, skin-side down, on the plate.

2. Combine the soy sauce, sesame oil, sugar, and vinegar in a bowl, then pour over the fish.

3. Scatter the ginger, chilli, and half the spring onions over the fish.

4. Set the steamer over a large saucepan or wok of simmering water and cover with the lid. Steam for 6 minutes or until the fish is opaque and just cooked.

5. Garnish the fish with coriander and the remaining spring onions, drizzle over the cooking juices from the plate, and serve with steamed rice.

Over 15 years ago, I discovered "Eat for your Blood Type" by Dr. Peter J. D'Adamo. It's a guideline on how to eat for your body and helps you understand why we need certain ingredients for fuel and wellness.

My husband is a B Type and craves lamb. It's what he needs to function well mentally and physically. This is one of his favourite meals and so easy to prepare.

Lamb and Lentil Salad

My Lamb and Lentil Salad with Yoghurt Dressing is a quick and delicious meal. Combining tender lamb with lentils, spinach, tomatoes and a zesty yoghurt dressing, it's perfect for any occasion. Yum!

Ingredients

1 tbsp olive oil
4 lamb fillets (140g each)
1 tsp smoked paprika
800g tinned brown lentils, drained and rinsed
2 tomatoes, chopped
1 bunch English spinach, ends trimmed, washed, dried, shredded
1 ½ tbsp fresh lemon juice
450g fat-reduced natural yoghurt
Sea salt and black pepper

Instructions

1. Rub the lamb fillets with 1 teaspoon of olive oil, smoked paprika, and a pinch of salt and pepper. Let them marinate for 30 minutes if you have time.

2. Heat remaining oil in a large non-stick frying pan over medium-high heat. Add the lamb and cook for 3 minutes on each side or until cooked to your liking. Transfer to a plate and cover loosely with foil to keep warm. Set aside to rest.

3. Add the lentils to the pan that you have cooked the lamb in, and toss gently for 2-3 minutes over medium heat until warmed through.

4. Add the tomatoes, spinach, and 1 tablespoon of lemon juice to the lentils and toss gently to combine. Taste and season with salt and pepper.

5. Thickly slice the lamb diagonally. Spoon the lentil mixture onto serving plates and top with the lamb slices.

6. Combine the remaining lemon juice and the yoghurt in a small bowl. Season with salt and pepper. Drizzle each salad with the yoghurt dressing.

Prepare
Your Week
Ahead

A few years ago I created a gluten-free catering service called Madame Foodie. The idea was to help our community fill their fridges with goodness and save time in the kitchen.

Life is busy and if you're not prepared, bad habits can form – especially around food. This can affect all areas of your life.

If you're keen to prepare for the week ahead and have the time, I recommend sitting down on the weekend to plan your meals.

Draw up the days of the week on paper and choose some delicious recipes from this book.

Write out your ingredients, go shopping, and prepare as much as possible on a Sunday. Control your week – don't let your week control you. You need to be prepared, and the rest will fall into place.

Don't put too much pressure on yourself to cook fancy three-course meals. Choose recipes that work for you and suit your family.

If you're serious about cooking, grocery shopping, and investing in high-quality produce, meat, and ingredients for the week, it's important to follow through with your commitment. Otherwise, you risk wasting both time and money and may end up feeling discouraged.

Stay focused and committed, and you'll be rewarded with delicious and satisfying meals that are worth the effort.

On the next pages you'll find my standard shopping list for a busy week as well as some meal planning worksheets to help you get organised! Make a copy of them and keep them in the kitchen to make planning simple.

My Top Tips:

Plan Ahead: Use a blank week plan to jot down your meals and shopping list.

Batch Cooking: Prepare larger portions and freeze them for quick meals during the week.

Stay Flexible: If something unexpected comes up, swap meals around to fit your schedule.

Kitchen Essentials

FRESH PRODUCE

Fresh fruits
Berries
Baby spinach
Rocket
Truss tomatoes
Carrots, zucchini, broccoli
Lemons, limes
Red onion, garlic, ginger
Spinach
Kale
Cauliflower
Eggplant
Fresh herbs

FRIDGE

Full-fat butter
Full-fat cream
Full-fat cheese
Free-range whole chicken
Barramundi or salmon
Free-range meat

PANTRY

Gluten-free flour
Gluten-free breadcrumbs
Polenta
Gluten-free stock cubes

Spices: cumin, smoked paprika,
cinnamon, coriander, curry powder
Gluten-free pasta

Rice: arborio, brown rice, basmati
Coconut cream
Tamari
Sesame oil
Olive oil
Tinned tomatoes
Sea salt or Himalayan salt
Tinned tuna
Raw honey
Gluten-free Vegemite

Meal Planner

FROM: / / TO: / /

	BREAKFAST	LUNCH	DINNER	SNACKS
MON				
TUE				
WED				
THU				
FRI				
SAT				
SUN				

GROCERY SHOPPING LIST

○ _____   ○ _____   ○ _____

○ _____   ○ _____   ○ _____

○ _____   ○ _____   ○ _____

○ _____   ○ _____   ○ _____

○ _____   ○ _____   ○ _____

Shopping List

MEAT / FISH / DAIRY	QTY

FRUITS & VEGETABLES	QTY

PANTRY ITEMS	QTY

FREEZER ITEMS	QTY

DRINKS & SNACKS	QTY

MISCELLANEOUS	QTY

Nourishing with Soups

There's nothing quite as comforting as a pot of soup simmering on the stove, especially on a rainy day.

A steaming bowl of soup feels like a warm hug in a bowl!

Soups can be filling, delicious, and nourishing, making them perfect for a light dinner or lunch.

I really have so many favourites that I would like to share with you, but here are my absolute TOP 5 recipes.

Vegetable & Chickpea Soup

This soup is self-care in a bowl. Make it on a Sunday to have in your fridge all week, to enjoy for lunch, a snack, or a light dinner. This super healthy and delicious soup is packed with so much goodness!

Ingredients

1 onion, diced
2 cloves garlic, diced
2 carrots, diced
2 celery sticks, diced
2 zucchinis, diced
1 handful of beans,
chopped into 3cm pieces
1 head of broccoli,
chopped into pieces
1 small head of cauliflower,
chopped into pieces
1 tbsp olive oil
1 litre chicken stock
1 tin of chickpeas
½ bunch parsley
1 lemon
Sea salt and black pepper

Instructions

1. Wash and chop all the vegetables.

2. Place a pot on the stovetop and drizzle in a tablespoon of olive oil. Heat on medium heat. Add garlic and onion. Stir until aromatic.

3. Pour in chicken stock and an additional cup of water.

4. Throw in all vegetables. Place a lid on the pot and simmer for 30 minutes until tender.

5. Add chickpeas, parsley, and a squeeze of lemon. Season to taste with salt and pepper.

6. You can leave the soup chunky or blend – up to you. Enjoy a healthy helping, then place the rest in containers and freeze them to take to work or for snacks and lunch.

Super Green Quinoa Soup

This soup has more protein than a chicken breast! The protein comes from quinoa, which is a complete protein, as it contains all nine essential amino acids that our bodies cannot produce on their own. It's an underrated grain that gives so much more than we know!

Ingredients

2 cups of cooked quinoa
½ bunch of spinach
1 cup of frozen peas
2 zucchinis, chopped
½ onion, chopped
2 cloves of garlic, sliced
1 bok choy
500ml chicken stock
Squeeze of lemon

Instructions

1. Cook the quinoa following the packet instructions. Drain and set aside.

2. Throw everything in a pot except the quinoa and lemon. Bring to a boil and simmer until veggies are cooked.

3. Blend the mixture until smooth.

4. Add cooked quinoa and a squeeze of lemon.

5. Serve in deep bowls. You can add some chilli to your liking and I also love to add some Parmesan cheese!

Red Curried Lentil Soup

This will get your bowels moving! We all need to be more consistent with our number twos! Lentils are packed with fibre to create the motion. You can adjust the curry flavour to your liking.

Ingredients

1 tbsp olive oil
1 large onion, chopped
3 cloves of garlic, finely diced
2 tbsp fresh ginger,
finely grated
1 ½ tbsp curry powder
1 tsp cinnamon
1 tsp ground cumin
1 ½ cups red lentils, rinsed
2 litres chicken stock
3 tbsp chopped coriander
2 tbsp lemon juice
Unsweetened yoghurt

Instructions

1. Heat the oil in a heavy stockpot over medium heat. Add the onion and sauté until softened for 3 to 5 minutes.

2. Add the garlic, ginger, curry powder, cinnamon, and cumin. Cook, stirring, for about 5 minutes longer.

3. Stir in the lentils and stock and bring to a boil. Reduce heat to low and simmer, partially covered, until the lentils are soft (about 20-25 minutes).

4. Stir in the coriander and lemon juice. Season with salt and pepper.

5. Ladle the soup into bowls and garnish with yoghurt.

Beef & Quinoa Stew

This is a hearty stew for the males of my household. I love smelling the flavours as the stew bubbles away on the stovetop. This is pure comfort food and guaranteed to bring the whole family to the table!

Ingredients

1 tbsp olive oil
1 large onion, diced
500g beef chuck steak, trimmed and cut into 3cm pieces
4 medium carrots, chopped
4 stalks celery, chopped
5 garlic cloves, finely diced
1.25 litres of beef stock
½ cup tomato passata
1 cup (200g) uncooked quinoa

Instructions

1. Heat a large pot over medium heat. Coat the pan with olive oil, add chopped onion and beef to the pan, and cook for 10 minutes or until the onions are tender and the beef is browned, stirring occasionally.

2. Add chopped carrot and celery to the pan, then cook for 5 minutes, stirring occasionally.

3. Stir in the garlic and cook for 30 seconds.

4. Add the stock, passata and 3 cups of water. Stir in quinoa and bring to the boil. Cover, reduce heat, and simmer for 40 minutes or until the quinoa is done and the beef is tender.

5. Serve in a large bowl and provide a large spoon!

Asian Broth with Whole Chicken

This is one of the simplest mid-week meals that everyone will adore. Asian recipes don't always require a hundred ingredients, which often deters us from cooking this cuisine due to the numerous steps and ingredients involved. Honestly, you'll make this once a week and fall in love with it!

Ingredients

¼ cup of sesame oil
1 onion, diced
4 cloves of garlic, diced
2 carrots, diced
2 sticks of celery, diced
2 zucchinis, diced
2 tbsp of five spice
1 whole chicken, free range
(2kg – 2.4kg)
½ cup (125ml) of tamari
1 chicken stock cube
1 tbsp chopped ginger
1 packet of rice noodles (200g)
Optional extras:
coriander and lemon

Instructions

1. Heat the sesame oil in a soup pot, then add all vegetables and fry off with five spice.

2. Add the chicken and cover with 2 litres of water. Bring to the boil, then reduce heat to a simmer. Add tamari, stock cube, and ginger and cook for an hour.

3. Once cooked, take out the chicken and shred it, then place the chicken back into the pot. Add the rice noodles.

4. Once the noodles are cooked (approx. 5 minutes), it's ready to be served.

5. Serve in large bowls with coriander and lemon.

Fancy Pancy Dinner Parties

I've been hosting dinner parties since my early twenties.

There's nothing I love more than seeing our large family table surrounded with friends and family enjoying good food.

My style is always to serve large platters in the middle of the table for everyone to help themselves from and yes – often over-eat!

I have some favourite impressive dishes, but the problem (and blessing) is we've had the same set of friends for over 30 years now, so I need to mix it up occasionally.

Scott always laughs when I start setting the table first thing in the morning on the day of entertaining. But I just love knowing that the table is set and ready to go. It honestly makes me happy to set each plate alongside cotton napkins, cutlery, wine glasses, fresh flowers, and candles.

My tip: Make sure you have everything ready before your guests arrive. The more you do it, the more you'll love it.

These recipes are all super easy but just a little fancy, with minimal effort to impress whoever you please – including yourself!

And the best part is that your guests won't even know they are eating gluten-free.

Tandoori Chicken Sticks

This is a fun recipe to serve as a starter!
The presentation is stunning with the creamy minted yoghurt and the bright orange skewer ready to be enjoyed. Perfect for a summer afternoon with a glass of Rosé.

Ingredients

Juice of 1 lemon
2 garlic cloves
1 tsp ground cumin seeds
2 tsp ground coriander seeds
1 tsp turmeric
2 tbsp paprika
Pinch of salt
500g chicken breasts, diced
1 tbsp olive oil
200g coconut yoghurt
1 Lebanese cucumber, grated
1 garlic clove, finely chopped
A small bunch of fresh mint

Instructions

1. In a food processor, blend lemon juice, garlic, all spices and salt.

2. Pour the mixture over the chicken pieces and marinate for 15-30 minutes.

3. Thread the chicken pieces onto skewers.

4. Cook on a hot BBQ for 10 minutes, turning every couple of minutes. Drizzle with oil halfway through cooking.

5. To make the minted yoghurt, combine the coconut yoghurt, grated cucumber, chopped garlic, and finely chopped mint. Stir well.

6. Serve the hot skewers with the minted yoghurt on the side and enjoy!

7. For a fun twist, use short bamboo skewers and serve with the minted yoghurt in shot glasses.

Crispy Chinese Pork Belly

This is a great starter for dinner parties, but I also make a big batch during holidays and keep it in the fridge for the kids. It's a tasty, filling option that beats a packet of chips or sugary snacks. Easy to reheat in a frypan or enjoy cold, it's a real crowd-pleaser!

Ingredients

1.25kg pork belly
2 tsp five spice
3 tbsp sesame oil
2 tsp sesame seeds
½ cup tamari
2 tsp grated ginger
1 green onion, sliced
Red chilli, sliced
Asian greens, steamed
Cooked basmati rice or rice noodles to serve

Instructions

1. Rub the pork with five spice, sesame oil, and sesame seeds. Leave uncovered for 30 minutes in the fridge.

2. Preheat the oven to 220°C / 425°F / Gas 7.

3. Place the pork with the skin side up on a baking tray lined with baking paper. Cook for 10 minutes, then reduce heat to 180°C / 350°F / Gas 4 and cook for a further 1.5 hours.

4. Take the pork out of the oven and allow it to rest for 10 minutes before cutting into pieces. You can choose bite-sized pieces or larger pieces to serve.

5. To make the sauce, combine the tamari, grated ginger, green onion and sliced chilli.

6. Dip pork bites in the sauce or drizzle with the sauce and serve with rice and steamed greens.

73

To serve, cut large squid hoods in half or quarters and serve on the sweet potato mash. Pour over the sauce, add some extra feta, and sprinkle with fresh herbs.

Serve with pan-fried greens such as beans, broccoli, and spinach.

You can also use smaller squid (pictured) and serve two per person.

Stuffed Squid with Brown Rice

This is my ultimate dinner party dish! Why? It sounds so fancy, looks incredible when served, and tastes amazing. You can prepare it all in advance and keep it in the fridge ready to go before your guests arrive. Then, once in the oven, it will cook away beautifully and be ready when you are.

Ingredients

2 large pieces of squid hood (approx. 250g–300g per hood)
Handful of toothpicks or skewers
2 cups of brown or white rice, cooked
½ cup of pitted dates
100g of feta cheese, plus an additional 100g for serving
1 bottle of passata (1 litre)
1 red onion, diced
4 garlic cloves, diced
Fresh cherry tomatoes
1 cup red wine
(and 1 cup for you!)
Fresh herbs: parsley & basil
2 large sweet potatoes, diced (approx. 1kg)
50g butter

Instructions

1. Preheat the oven to 180°C / 350°F / Gas 4.

2. Combine the cooked rice, diced onion, garlic, chopped dates, and herbs.

3. Place each squid hood on a chopping board and secure one ends with toothpicks.

4. Fill the squid with the stuffing mixture, then secure the other end with toothpicks and place in a baking dish.

5. Pour the passata over the squid, crumble over the feta cheese, place cherry tomatoes on top, sprinkle with salt, add 1 cup red wine, and cover with tin foil.

6. Bake covered for 45 minutes, then remove the foil and cook for a further 15 minutes.

7. Meanwhile, bring a pot of water to boil and cook the sweet potatoes. Once cooked through, mash and add butter and salt to taste.

When I first started catering 25 years ago, I was in search of show stoppers to impress a crowd. This was it!

I had never cooked a whole fish before, and the thought of it intimidated me.

However, once I realised how simple the steps were, it became the highlight of my catering menu as well as our home dinner table.

Baked Whole Fish with Sticky Sauce

This dish is so easy yet so fancy. Serve it on a large platter as part of a buffet or in the middle of your family table. Ask your fishmonger to clean and scale it. Slit down the middle so you can stuff the fish with fresh lemon. Yes, keep the head and tail on – it's the best part!

Ingredients

3kg whole fish (snapper or barramundi)
3 lemons, quartered
1 shallot, diced
½ cup sesame oil for fish
¼ cup sesame oil for frying
2 garlic cloves, grated
1 small piece of ginger, grated
2 long chillies, finely chopped
¾ cup palm sugar
½ cup fish sauce
⅓ cup lime juice
4 cups cooked Basmati rice
½ can coconut cream
Fresh limes to serve
2 tbsp sesame seeds
1 bunch fresh coriander or Thai basil, roughly chopped
Banana leaves

Instructions

1. Preheat the oven to 200°C / 400°F / Gas 6.

2. Place the fish on a large piece of baking paper. Drizzle with sesame oil and stuff the lemons and shallot in the middle of the fish. Then wrap in foil and cook for 1 hour.

3. In a wok, heat ¼ cup of sesame oil. Add garlic, ginger, and chilli, then add palm sugar, fish sauce and lime juice. Bring to a boil, then simmer for 10 minutes until it thickens. Add more lime juice to taste, then transfer to a jug and set aside.

4. Meanwhile, cook the rice as per packet instructions. Once cooked, drain and stir in ½ can of coconut cream. Leave to absorb.

5. To check if the fish is cooked is to remove the wrapping and gently slice open the thickest part of the fish. It should be perfectly white and flake easily.

6. Once cooked, transfer the fish to a large platter lined with banana leaves. Place fresh lime halves around the fish. Sprinkle over sesame and herbs and serve with coconut rice.

Whole Baked Salmon

with Coconut & Basil Pesto

Salmon is a bit more expensive than white fish, but definitely worth the investment for a special occasion. The contrast between the light pink colour of the salmon and the fragrant green pesto is truly gorgeous.

Ingredients

1 whole salmon – approx. 2kg, ask your fishmonger to scale and clean
2 lemons, cut in half
2 tbsp olive oil
1kg white potatoes, cut into chunks (approx. 6cm)
2 tbsp oregano

COCONUT BASIL PESTO:
500ml coconut cream
1 bunch of basil
3 garlic cloves
½ red onion
Juice of ½ lemon
2 tbsp olive oil
2 pinches of sea salt

Instructions

1. Preheat the oven to 200°C / 400°F / Gas 6.

2. Place the whole salmon on large sheets of tin foil to eventually wrap it in. Stuff the salmon with the lemon halves. Drizzle with 1 tablespoon of olive oil and sprinkle with salt. Wrap in foil securely and place on an oven tray.

3. Cut the potatoes into chunks, toss in the remaining olive oil and dried oregano, and roast in the oven on a lined baking tray for one hour.

4. Cook the salmon in the preheated oven for 1 hour. Check after 45 minutes by using a fork – if the salmon flakes, it's cooked. Be careful of the steam when opening the foil.

5. In a food processor, add coconut cream, fresh basil, garlic, red onion, a squeeze of lemon juice, and approx. 2 tbsp olive oil. Blend to form a pesto.

6. Place the salmon on a large white platter. Remove the skin if you prefer, or slice into the middle allowing the pesto to seep through. Drizzle with the pesto and serve with the roasted potatoes.

Sunday Night Family Dinners

Mid-week dinners have become nearly impossible since the kids are growing into young adults. You will often find just two or three of us sitting at the kitchen bench, with the rest of the family floating in at some point due to uni, sport, or work.

About a year ago, we all committed unintentionally that Sunday would be our family dinner night. At first, it just happened, then we loved it, and now it's do or die to be at the table come Sunday dinner time.

I usually start cooking at 4pm to prepare those family feasts, as we have big kids to feed, including Pringle, Hanna's boyfriend, who plays professional AFL.

We all love tradition and routine. And it's essential to make those commitments to keep them up.

Here are some of my family favourites.

Italian Chicken Schnitzels

Be warned – you might need to make double this recipe. I always think I have made enough and never do! Not only for seconds at the dinner table, but also to have in the fridge for a midnight snack or lunch the next day.
Pringle (the boyfriend) could eat four in one sitting!

Ingredients

4 chicken breasts (200g each)
4 slices of prosciutto
12 basil leaves
125g fresh mozzarella, sliced
250g gluten-free flour
2 free-range eggs, beaten
2 cups gluten-free breadcrumbs (store-bought or homemade from gluten-free bread)
Olive oil for cooking (approx. 2 cups)

Instructions

1. Preheat the oven to 180°C / 350°F / Gas 4.

2. Make a pocket in each chicken breast by slicing open the middle part of the breast enough to stuff with prosciutto, basil, and mozzarella.

3. Dust the stuffed breasts in flour, then dip in the whisked eggs and coat with breadcrumbs. Set these up in three bowls alongside each other for easy dipping.

4. Heat a frypan with 1 cup of olive oil. To test if the oil is hot enough, place a small cube of bread in the oil – if it sizzles, it's ready! Pan-fry each side for approx. 2 minutes until light golden brown.

5. Transfer to a lined baking tray and bake in the oven for about 20 minutes or until cooked. It's always best to slice into the thickest part of the chicken – if it's see-through in colour, pop it back in the oven until completely white and cooked through.

6. Serve with a large green salad and sweet potato fries.

Super Tasty Chicken Drumsticks

Every week, I cook a large batch of drumsticks for the fridge. It's easy for the kids to walk past, open the fridge (which they do 500 times a day!), and grab one on the go. Much better than a packet of chips. Good protein snack. Tasty!

Ingredients

12 chicken drumsticks (approx. 200g each)
2 tbsp tomato sauce
1 tbsp olive oil
1 tbsp tamari
1 tbsp honey
1 tsp curry powder
1 tsp paprika
2 tbsp sesame seeds
Small bunch of fresh parsley

Instructions

1. Cut slashes in the sides of the drumsticks and add them to a bowl with all the other ingredients. Marinate for 30 minutes.

2. Preheat the oven to 220°C / 425°F / Gas 7.

3. Place the drumsticks on a cooking tray lined with baking paper. Bake in the preheated oven for about 30-40 minutes. The drumsticks will look crispy and colourful.

4. Slice into the thickest part to ensure the drumstick is cooked through before serving.

5. Sprinkle with sesame seeds and parsley to garnish.

Easy Chilli Baked Fish

You are going to love this dish! Not only because it takes no effort, but because it's so delicious that you will want to eat it every day of the week! The combination of flavours is a match made in heaven.

Ingredients

1 garlic clove
2 spring onions, sliced
1 tbsp lemongrass
1 tsp turmeric
3 tbsp sweet chilli sauce
2 tbsp lemon juice
1 tbsp fresh coriander
1 cup coconut cream
4 fillets of fresh white fish
2 tbsp cashews, chopped

Instructions

1. Preheat the oven to 190°C / 375°F / Gas 5.

2. In a food processor, blend the garlic, spring onions, lemongrass, turmeric, sweet chilli sauce, lemon juice, and fresh coriander until smooth. Stir in the coconut cream.

3. Place the fish in a baking dish and cover with the coconut cream mixture. Cover the dish with foil and cook for 30 minutes.

4. Serve with rice noodles or basmati rice, and steamed green vegetables such as beans, broccoli, or bok choy. Add more chilli to your liking and sprinkle with extra coriander and cashews for a little crunch.

Lamb & Eggplant Burgers

This is a fabulous summer family meal. You have a choice of iceberg lettuce cups if you are keeping your carbs low at night or a gluten-free burger bun for a more substantial dinner. The gluten-free buns are delicious when toasted, which you can coordinate just before serving.

Ingredients

CAPSICUM PUREE
2 capsicums, roasted
2 garlic cloves, roasted
2 tbsp olive oil
1 chilli, finely chopped
2 tsp red wine vinegar

LAMB BURGERS
1kg lamb mince
½ cup pine nuts
1 garlic clove, crushed
1 tsp cinnamon
½ cup parsley, chopped
1 tsp lemon zest
1 egg
2 eggplants, cut into 1cm thick slices
Iceberg lettuce or burger buns
Greek yoghurt (optional)

Instructions

1. Place capsicums and garlic in a foil parcel with 2 tablespoons of olive oil. Wrap to secure. Place in a 200°C / 400°F / Gas 6 oven for 30 minutes. Open the parcel, allow the steam to escape and cool.

2. Place lamb mince, pine nuts, garlic, cinnamon, parsley, lemon zest and egg in a bowl, mix with your hands and then make 4 generous patties.

3. Grill the patties and eggplant slices on a preheated BBQ for 10 minutes, turning every 2 minutes to cook evenly. Alternatively, bake in a preheated oven at 180°C / 350°F / Gas 4 on a lined tray for approx. 15 minutes. When you pierce the patty with a knife, the juice should run clear.

4. Place the capsicum ingredients into a blender and blitz until pureed. Add sea salt to taste.

5. Build your burger with the patty, eggplant slice, and capsicum puree. Greek yoghurt is another lovely addition to dollop on the patty.

6. Serve with homemade wedges.

Coriander Pork Dumplings

with rice noodles and Asian broth

For years, I have been teaching Gluten-Free Cooking Classes. It's a true love of mine to educate others on how easy and simple gluten-free recipes can be when shown my way. This is one of my all-time favourite cooking class recipes, which the crowds love!

Ingredients

1 litre chicken stock
500g pork mince
2 garlic cloves, chopped
1 tbsp grated ginger
1 tbsp fish sauce
A small bunch of fresh coriander, chopped
2 carrots
2 zucchinis
1 red capsicum
2 cups green peas
¼ cup tamari
4 tbsp sesame oil
1 packet of rice noodles (500g)
Bean sprouts to garnish

Instructions

1. Bring a large pot of stock mixed with 1 litre of water to the boil.

2. Blend garlic, ginger, fish sauce, coriander, 1 carrot, and 1 zucchini. Add this to a bowl along with the pork mince. Mix with your hands and create small dumplings – just under the size of a golf ball. Place aside.

3. Cut up the additional carrot, zucchini, and capsicum into bite-sized pieces. Add to the stock.

4. When the stock is boiling, reduce heat to a simmer and add the pork dumplings. Add tamari, sesame oil, and the noodles and cook for five to ten minutes. The dumplings will float to the top.

5. Once the dumplings and noodles are cooked, serve in bowls with bean sprouts on top and extra coriander.

Beef Kofta Board with Hummus

and homemade Tabouli

Ingredients

KOFTAS:
1kg beef mince
1 bunch parsley, chopped
1 red onion, finely diced
2 tsp each of cumin, coriander, and paprika
Pinch of sea salt

HUMMUS:
1 tin of chickpeas
½ cup lemon juice
3 garlic cloves
2 tsp salt
1 cup tahini
Drizzle of olive oil

TABOULI:
½ cup chopped mint
3 bunches chopped parsley
1 bunch spring onions, sliced
3 large tomatoes, diced
½ cup olive oil
Juice of ½ lemon
1 cup cooked quinoa

Instructions

1. To make the Koftas: Mix all ingredients together and form into sausage-shaped koftas (approx. the length and width of your thumb). Place on a lined oven tray, spray with olive oil, and sprinkle with salt. Preheat oven to 180°C / 350°F / Gas 4 and bake for 30 minutes.

2. To make the Hummus: Blend chickpeas, lemon juice, garlic, salt, tahini, and a drizzle of olive oil. Serve in a small bowl on the board.

3. To make the Tabouli: In a large bowl, combine mint, parsley, spring onions, tomatoes, olive oil, lemon juice, and quinoa. Toss together.

4. On a large wooden board, place the koftas in one section, hummus in a bowl, and tabouli in a bowl. Add fresh lemon wedges and sliced chilli. Provide small bowls for people to help themselves.

I love any excuse for our family to be together, and of course, I will always bring food to the table as the enticement!

This is a communal dish where you place the board in the middle of the table and let everyone help themselves. You can serve with gluten-free wraps or rice, or just as is.

Mum, I'm hungry... at 3pm!

It's the story of my life!

I have spoilt the kids by always making healthy food for them to eat.

Chips and sugary or salty snacks are expensive and are never the best option to fill hungry tummies. Sure, it's OK to have them in the cupboard, however, if you want your kids to learn to eat properly, you need to have some other, healthier options available.

Especially at 3pm, which seems to be the hungry hour!

My Nonna's Bolognese Recipe

As promised, I am sharing our family recipe! This is the most delicious food option to constantly have in your fridge. You can add it to pasta, rice, serve on toast, or have just on its own. It's perfect for the 3pm craving and also healthy! My advice is to cook this on a Sunday afternoon ready for the week.

Ingredients

1kg pork mince
1kg beef mince
2 red onions, diced
4 garlic cloves, diced
2 cups red wine
500ml passata
Sea salt and black pepper

Instructions

1. In a large pot on medium heat, drizzle 2 tbsp olive oil, add onions and garlic. Stir until you can smell the amazing aromas combining.

2. Add both types of mince and break up any large chunks. Brown the meat slightly to create flavour.

3. Pour in the wine and bring to a simmer.

4. Stir in the passata and a good pinch of salt. Continue to simmer for 10 minutes.

5. Reduce the heat to low and cook for as long as you can – minimum 45 minutes, maximum 4 hours.

6. Continue to taste and add salt and pepper to your liking. Add ½ cup of water if the sauce becomes too thick.

7. Let the sauce cool and enjoy with your family!

Sesame Chicken Rice Paper Rolls

My Sesame Chicken Rice Paper Rolls are perfect for an after-school snack. They're packed with tasty veggies and juicy chicken, all wrapped up in rice paper or alternatively in crunchy baby cos lettuce cups. Quick to make and fun to eat, they'll become a favourite in no time!

Ingredients

1 tbsp sesame oil
1 tbsp ginger, minced
1 tbsp garlic, minced
150g chicken mince
1 cup peas
1 carrot, diced
1 capsicum, diced
Dash of tamari to taste
1 tin of bamboo shoots (drained)
½ cup coriander, chopped
1 packet rice paper, or 3–4 baby cos lettuce

Instructions

1. In a frypan, heat sesame oil, ginger, and garlic. Stir for 1-2 minutes on medium heat. Add the chicken mince and break it up with a fork. Once cooked, add all vegetables except coriander and lettuce. Add a dash of tamari, bamboo shoots, and coriander, and remove from the heat.

2. Fill a large bowl with warm water. Dip one rice paper sheet into the water for about 5 seconds to soften.

3. Lay the softened rice paper on a flat surface. Place a small amount of the chicken mixture in the centre of the rice paper.

4. Fold the bottom edge of the rice paper over the filling. Fold in the sides, then roll up tightly from the bottom to the top. Repeat with the remaining rice paper sheets and filling.

5. Serve with a dipping sauce of your choice. If you're not using rice paper, spoon the filling into baby cos lettuce leaves instead and serve like san choy bow.

Gluten-Free Banana Bread

Everyone loves Banana Bread! I love to bake it during the day and enjoy the aroma of banana, cinnamon, and vanilla wafting through the house. It's homely. Once baked, I leave it to cool on the island bench and then slice it for the kids to grab on their way through.

Ingredients

1 ⅔ cups wholemeal, gluten-free flour
1 ½ tsp baking powder
⅓ cup raw sugar
1 tsp cinnamon
1 tsp vanilla essence
½ cup apple juice
3 mashed bananas
Olive oil spray, for the tin

Instructions

1. Place the dry ingredients in a bowl and make a well in the centre. Add the apple juice and mashed bananas. Mix until combined.

2. Pour the mixture into a loaf tin that has been sprayed with olive oil (this is an important step, otherwise it's very frustrating trying to release the bread from the tin later).

3. Bake in the oven at 160°C / 320°F / Gas 3 for 60 minutes or until cooked.

4. Insert a skewer into the middle of the banana bread. If it comes out clean, it's cooked. If it has mixture attached, it needs to bake a little longer.

5. Take it out of the oven and place it on a wire tray to cool. When cool, store in the fridge, as there are no preservatives!

Old School Popcorn

Heat a pot with
3 tablespoons of olive oil.

Once hot, add half a cup of
popcorn kernels.

Put the lid on and let the
kernels pop away.

In a saucepan,
melt 3 tablespoons of butter
and 3 tablespoons of honey,
then drizzle on the popcorn.

Enjoy!

Sweet Potato Chips

Slice a sweet potato and toss it in olive oil and sea salt.

Place the slices on an oven tray lined with baking paper.

Bake at
220°C / 425°F / Gas 7
for approximately 20 minutes.

Let cool and dig in!

Cheeky
gluten Free
Treats

I am definitely not a baker! I don't really believe in measurements, but they are important to achieve reliable baking results.

Therefore, I have included some easy dessert recipes. They don't require too much precision, but still taste amazing. I know you are going to love this sweet gluten-free inspiration.

Here are my top favs!

Baked Egg Custard

This is the easiest dessert that I always used to make for the kids when they were little. It's definitely their comfort food.
Now as they are young adults, when they know I am cooking this old favourite, they come running and ask for seconds!

Ingredients

6 egg yolks
2.5 cups full cream milk
1 cup thickened cream
1/3 cup raw sugar
1 tsp vanilla extract
Cinnamon to sprinkle

Instructions

1. Preheat the oven to 180°C / 350°F / Gas 4.

2. Place egg yolks, cream, milk, sugar, and vanilla in a bowl and whisk well. Pour into a medium-sized ceramic baking dish.

3. Bake in the oven for 25 minutes. The custard will become firm yet still wobble. Take out of the oven to cool for 10 minutes.

4. Sprinkle cinnamon on top and serve in bowls or eat straight from the dish! This custard can be enjoyed warm or cold.

Caramel Apple with Maple Syrup

The combination of apples, butter and sugar is all you need to create a delicious homely dessert. We call it "cooked apple" at home and it's another comfort food for the family, especially on a rainy day after school or work. It's so easy to make and enjoyable!

Ingredients

50g butter
1 tbsp brown sugar
1 tbsp maple syrup
1 tsp cinnamon
3 green apples, peeled and chopped into pieces (I tend to chop into square shapes)

Instructions

1. Place a frypan on the stovetop over medium heat. Combine butter, syrup, sugar, and cinnamon in a small saucepan.

2. Allow the mixture to heat through and bubble slightly, not intensely as you don't want the sugar to burn.

3. Toss apples through the butter mixture and cook for 10 minutes on a gentle heat to soften. The sauce will become sticky.

4. Serve warm with custard, mascarpone, or ice cream – or all three!

Coconut Ice Cream Balls

A simple dessert is always appreciated by the host and the guests. Quite often we are so full after a meal that we only need a mouthful of something sweet to finish our fabulous feast. This recipe will be your new dessert when entertaining. Not only because it's so simple, but because it's so delicious!

Ingredients

2–3 cups desiccated coconut
2 litres of rich vanilla ice cream
½ cup flaked coconut

Instructions

1. Place desiccated coconut on a flat tray. Line a couple of oven trays with baking paper.

2. Use an ice cream scoop and a melon baller to make different sized balls of ice cream. Place the balls in the coconut and gently roll to cover. Place on tray. Cover with cling wrap. Freeze for 2-3 hours.

3. To serve, place the ice cream balls in a martini glass, sprinkled with flaked coconut and topped with berries.

Chilled Chocolate Torte

Hello chocolate lovers! This torte is worth the small effort to create. Trust me! With only 5 ingredients, it's simple but too good to be true. You'll totally wow your guests at the end of the meal, so maybe make two, just to be safe!

Ingredients

300g milk chocolate
1/3 cup raw sugar (40g)
3 egg yolks
1 egg
600ml thickened cream

Instructions

1. Break the chocolate into pieces and blend in a food processor until finely chopped.

2. Heat the sugar and 150ml of water over medium heat, stirring until the sugar has melted. Increase the heat and boil for 2 minutes until it slightly thickens.

3. With the food processor running, pour the hot sugar syrup into the chocolate. Add the egg yolks and egg, and process until well blended. Let the mixture cool slightly.

4. Whip the cream to soft peaks. Then gently fold the chocolate mixture through the whipped cream until well combined.

5. Grease a 22cm cake tin and line it with baking paper. Pour the mixture into the cake tin.

6. Freeze for at least 4 hours or (better overnight!) Leave out for 20 minutes before serving. Just before you serve, dust with cocoa powder or grated chocolate and serve with fresh berries.

Wreath of Happiness

This festive wreath is my absolute favourite to serve at any time of the day and also to take to parties. As you know by now, I like simple recipes, and this one is as easy as pouring your first glass of festive champagne!

Ingredients

1 packet of gluten-free chocolate biscuits
600ml thickened cream
3 tbsp vanilla essence
Fresh berries (strawberries, blueberries, raspberries, etc.)
Flake chocolate

Instructions

1. Whip the cream and vanilla essence until thick.

2. Set up a large round plate. Spread cream on one side of a biscuit, then press it together with the next biscuit.

3. Continue spreading cream and pressing biscuits together to form a circle. Make sure to press the biscuits tightly together to build a strong foundation.

4. Once your circle is complete, spread the remaining cream on top of the wreath.

5. Place fresh berries on top and break up flake chocolate to scatter over.

6. Place in the fridge to set for at least an hour. Then, slice and serve with additional whipped cream or even custard!

First and foremost, thank you to my family:

Scott, Han, Kye and Lu.

Always being supportive of my dreams. Working around a
messy home kitchen when practicing recipes.
Loving all the leftovers!

I do this all for you.

My Besties! I have a beautiful handful of girlfriends who have
been around for over 45 years. They are my confidants who
listen, guide and support.

Thank you for listening to my crazy ideas and making them
sound completely normal. You are my sanity whether we are
sitting over a glass a wine or a coffee. Friendships forever!

Melinda, my Energy Healer, I have to mention you! You are so
much more than this! You are have been my advisor for years
and guiding me to the best choices with clarity and belief.
Thank you.

Ben and Pam! You made this happen! For years, you have been telling me to connect with Jay and Max. I was nervous and hesitant to take the first step. Thank you for pushing me into this direction.

Yes, I know, I owe you lunch!

Jay and Max, where do I start! Thank you for taking me on as part of your "Cookbook Family" and being so patient in a world that is completely new.

The belief you have in me, is overwhelming. I am eternally grateful that we worked on this project for over 3 years and how the process has just fallen into place effortlessly. This book is the first of many. I cant wait to let this adventure unfold.

Jay, you have taken these recipes from my head and vision and photographed them to perfection! We eat with our eyes and you have nailed my dream of my cookbook being a beautiful visual to encourage people to cook! I'm in awe of your talent!

Luka Rayment, the talented photographer who has captured the cover and my family shots through the book. You are truly amazing with a very bright future in front of you.

Thank you for bringing to life, my life.

x Raquel

Index

Index

Notes

....

....

....

....

....

....

....

....

....

....

....

....

....

....

....

....

....

Notes

Here's to good food And good health!

THANK YOU FOR JOINING ME ON THIS COOKING ADVENTURE!
IF YOU'RE HUNGRY FOR MORE DELICIOUS RECIPE INSPIRATION,
VISIT ME ME ONLINE!

WWW.LIVEWELLBYRAQUEL.COM

INSTAGRAM
@LIVEWELLBYRAQUEL

This cookbook is intended for individuals following a gluten-free diet. Every effort has been made to ensure that the ingredients and preparation methods used in these recipes contain no detectable gluten. However, it is essential to always check ingredient labels and be aware of potential cross-contamination risks. For those with coeliac disease, please consult with a healthcare professional if you have any concerns.

Milton Keynes UK
Ingram Content Group UK Ltd.
UKHW050853121224
452350UK00018B/179

9 783910 841048